Contents

Warning: Horrible habitats ahead!.... 2

Chapter 1: Extreme habitats............. 4

Chapter 2: Disgusting habitats 12

Chapter 3: Dangerous habitats 18

Chapter 4: Animal habitats 26

Chapter 5: Human habitats 32

Horrible habitats everywhere 36

Glossary 38

Index 39

Warning: Horrible habitats ahead!

Think of a habitat – a home for living things. A habitat must provide everything an animal needs, from food and water to shelter and **mates**.

Perhaps you're picturing …

- a lush rainforest
- a sunlit reef
- a cool ocean!

Think again! Many animals can find everything they need in a much smaller habitat. Some of these *habitats are horrible*.

Get ready to explore fiery volcanoes, stinky cowpats and snotty nostrils. Find out who lives in a toxic lake or a flesh - eating plant.

You'll even meet creatures that call your belly button home.

Now *this* is a horrible habitat!

Meet the neighbours

Every creature is part of an ecosystem – a community of living things that share a habitat. Look out for these boxes. They will introduce you to other members of each ecosystem.

Chapter 1: Extreme habitats

Space scientists say that Earth is a 'Goldilocks' planet. The **average** temperature around the world is 14°C. Just like the porridge in the fairy tale, this is not too hot nor too cold, but just right for life.

However, some habitats on Earth reach temperatures that would kill most living things.

121°C Deep-sea vent
100°C Water boils
80°C Hot spring
60°C Desert sand
0°C Water freezes
−2°C Polar ocean
−60°C Mount Everest in winter
−100°C Antarctica

Even in these extreme habitats, strange creatures survive.

Very hot habitats

The Sahara is the world's hottest desert. During the day, the sand heats up to 60°C. This would cook an egg – and most insects!

Saharan silver ants survive on this superheated sand. Their silvery hairs bounce sunlight away. Long legs keep their body off the sand and help them run fast. They feast on insects that have died in the heat.

Saharan silver ants

Very cold habitats

Did the last page make you long for an icy drink?

Some of the world's coldest water is found deep in the oceans around Antarctica. It is colder than ice, but the salt in the water stops it from freezing.

Antarctic blackfin icefish

Most fish would turn to ice if they swam here. Antarctic blackfin icefish can survive. They have special blood that does not freeze.

Antarctica's land is even colder than the sea! Penguins jump into the sea often to warm up. But some tiny Antarctic animals live their whole lives on land.

Water bears are tiny creatures that live in moss around the world, including Antarctica.

Water bear

Meet the Neighbours

These animals have different ways to survive in Antarctica.

Emperor penguins huddle together.

Orcas have a thick layer of **blubber**.

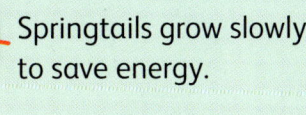

Springtails grow slowly to save energy.

Very high habitats

Mountains are Earth's highest habitats. They can get very cold, but this is not the only problem for living things.

Higher up, there is less air. This makes it difficult for animals to breathe.

8000 metres Humans die without an air supply

5500 metres The human body stops working properly

4000 metres Humans feel very ill

3000 metres Human senses stop working

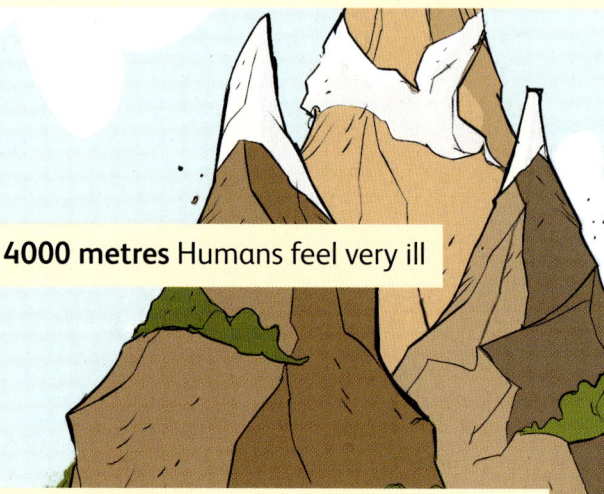

There are also fewer plants. Plants can only grow up to six kilometres above sea level. This means there is very little for animals to eat.

Himalayan jumping spiders have been found 6,700 metres up Mount Everest. They feed on insects that have been blown up the mountain.

Himalayan jumping spider

Mammals live near Mount Everest in the Himalayan mountains too. Himalayan wolves live more than 4,000 metres above sea level. Large-eared pika live more than 6,000 metres high, where wolves are less likely to reach them.

Large-eared pika

Very deep habitats

The deepest point on Earth's surface is the Mariana Trench. The bottom of this **trench** is 11 kilometres below the ocean surface.

Down here it is totally dark and very cold. However, visiting **submersibles** have photographed lots of creatures in this horrible habitat.

Giant isopods look like woodlice – if woodlice were 30 cm long! They eat dead creatures and droppings that sink down from the ocean above.

Deep-sea vents are hot springs on the ocean floor. The water rushing out has been heated by rocks deep in Earth's crust.

Pompeii worms live around the vents. They dangle their tails in water that is as hot as boiling water from a kettle! Do NOT try this at home, even if you have a tail. The worms are protected by a coat of germs that grow on their skin.

The germs make their own food using energy from the hot-water vents vents.

Then we worms eat the germs!

Chapter 2: Disgusting habitats

These habitats aren't too hot, too cold, too high or too low. But they are too disgusting for most living things!

Dead good

Many creatures steer clear of rotting plants and animals. Detritivores are different. They love to feed on dead things. For starters, dead animals are easier to catch!

Millipedes munch rotting leaves and wood.

Blowflies lay their eggs on dead animals.

Earthworms eat rotting plants and poop out soil.

Water springtails feed on dead flies and earthworms.

As they feed, detritivores help dead things to decay. They break down the dead things into materials that can then be used by other living things. There are detritivores in the ocean too. They are also known as 'bottom feeders'.

Sea cucumber

We eat dead things and animal droppings that sink to the bottom of the sea!

Urchin

⚠️ Delicious dung

When you think of the perfect home, a cowpat might be at the 'bottom' of your list! However, cowpats are habitats for living things too.

This hat-thrower fungus grows well in cowpats. There is plenty of food to eat – it's even been **digested** first!

To help it spread, the fungus makes **spores**, which need to get eaten by a new cow. Cows don't munch on their own poop, so the spores must escape the cowpat! To solve this problem, each fungus has a built-in water pistol!

The stalks slowly swell up with water – then explode! This pings the 'hat' (full of spores) more than two metres away on to fresh grass.

Lungworms are tiny worms that live inside cows. Their eggs get pooped out and hatch in cowpats.

To get themselves eaten by a new cow, the baby lungworms crawl up the stalk of a hat-thrower fungus, sit on the top …

It's a worm roller coaster!

… and wait to be launched on to fresh grass!

Hat-thrower fungus

Human habitats

Most disgusting of all are the habitats found near human beings.

Towns and cities are fully of noisy traffic, toxic pollution and stinky **sewage**.

Even in these horrible habitats, all kinds of animals find ways to survive.

Humans are so messy that food can be easy to find in a city. In many cities, pigeons peck food scraps off pavements, and seagulls circle landfill sites.

In Sydney, Australia, cockatoos open litter bins to steal snacks.

Not many humans would venture inside a sewer. But a surprising number of animals make their homes there.

For rats, sewers are dark and safe from **predators**. The rats use their whiskers to feel their way around. In the city of Barcelona, Spain, scientists counted 213,000 sewer rats.

 ## Meet the neighbours

These creatures also live in sewers:
- Sludge worms cling to sewer walls and eat anything that drifts past.
- Sometimes, snakes follow rats into drains and end up living in sewers!

Chapter 3: Dangerous habitats

Most creatures stay away from places where they might get bitten or stung. But there are creatures that hang out in these horrible habitats!

Sting zone

Wax moths sneak into beehives to lay their eggs. They risk getting stung, but for the moths the risk is worth it.

When their eggs hatch, the hungry caterpillars burrow through the honeycomb. They eat everything they find – beeswax, baby bees and even bee droppings!

Bee-licious!

Have you noticed how caterpillars happily hang out on stinging nettles? Scientists are trying to work out if they are **immune** to stings, or if they are just small enough to crawl between stinging hairs.

Anemones have dozens of stinging tentacles. Clownfish have found a way to live among them. The fish have a thick coating of slimy **mucus** that protects them from stings.

Toothy habitats

All habitats come with some risk of being eaten. But surely nothing would be daft enough to live inside a predator's mouth!

Meet the Egyptian plover. It shares its riverside habitat with crocodiles.

When a plover spots a crocodile with its jaws open, the bird flies right in!

It picks out and eats scraps of meat lodged in the crocodile's teeth!

The crocodile doesn't eat me because I'm its toothbrush!

Cleaner wrasse are small fish that live on **coral reefs**. When they spot a shark coming towards them ...

... with wide-open jaws ...

... they are not bothered. They swim right inside and pick scraps of food from between those terrible teeth. Sharks visit the wrasse to get their teeth cleaned!

Meet the neighbours

These animals also hang around sharks.
- Remoras and pilot fish nibble small creatures off the shark's skin.
- Tiny shrimps live in a whale shark's **gill**s, using their hairy legs to grab food.

wrasse

Don't get digested

Plants can be predators too! Pitcher plants digest small creatures that slide inside their long trumpets.

This might seem like a horrible habitat, but some bats roost in pitcher plants during the day!

The plant gives the bat a safe place to sleep, in return for the bat's droppings – which it collects and digests!

Not all pitcher plants make **digestive juices**. Some are filled with rainwater to drown victims. But animals that swim in water can live there!

Sometimes frogs lay their eggs in these pitcher plants. The tadpoles will hatch and grow in a place where predators dare not go.

 ### Meet the neighbours

These animals also hang around in pitcher plants:
- Crab spiders use silk to lower themselves in and grab something to eat.
- Some mosquitoes lay their eggs inside pitcher plants.
- Some ants live inside pitcher plants, stealing some of the trapped food for themselves.

⚠️ Toxic lakes

Watery places are usually teeming with life. However, some lakes are too salty or too toxic for most creatures to survive.

Not these sea monkeys! They are shrimps that love living in salty lakes, swamps and seas. Their gills help them to get rid of the extra salt that enters their bodies.

Lesser flamingo

Lesser flamingos live in toxic lakes in some parts of Africa. If you stood in the water, your skin would dissolve. The birds' tough skin and scales stop their legs getting burned.

The lakes are also home to tiny **microbes**. The flamingos eat the microbes!

Nothing else can stand and feed in these lakes, so the flamingos are safe.

This lake is in a volcano crater in Costa Rica. It's not just super salty. It's also acidic, toxic and hot! However, for a few types of microbes, it's home sweet home.

Chapter 4: Animal habitats

Animals live *in* habitats – but sometimes animals *are* habitats! Animals that live inside other animals without helping their host are known as **parasites**.

 ## Hidden passengers

Some of the most horrible habitats are found inside animals. This reindeer sinus worm lives its entire life snuggled up inside a reindeer's nostril!

Up there, the worm is warm and protected from predators. It can also eat as much snot as it wants!

No wonder reindeer get red noses!

If you think a reindeer's nostril is horrible, imagine living in a bee's bottom!

Stylops are tiny insects that lay their eggs inside wasps and bees. The baby stylops spend their whole lives inside the abdomens of wasps and bees. Look closely next time a wasp visits your picnicpicnic - you may you may see a small stylops poking out!

Zombie-makers

Some flatworms like to live inside a bird's **intestines** - but their young get pooped out! They need to get themselves eaten by a new bird, but birds don't eat bird poop.

However, snails do! Once the flatworm has been eaten by a snail, it sets up home in one of the snail's eyestalks. The eyestalk becomes bright and colourful, like a caterpillar.

A bird is tricked into eating this juicy 'caterpillar' and the life cycle begins again.

A horrible life cycle!

1. Snail eats poop
2. Flatworm grows in snail eyestalks
3. Bird eats snail
4. Bird poops on a leaf

Ants can be turned into zombies too.

One type of fungus infects carpenter ants. After using up the ant's energy, it takes over the ant's brain.

It makes the ant leave its nest and climb to the top of a plant. A small mushroom begins to grow out of the ant's head! The mushroom's spores rain to the ground and infect more ants.

⚠️ Even more horrible habitats

Parasitoid wasps might have the most horrible habitat of all.

These wasps start by stinging their victim, so it stays still.

Then they lay their eggs on the victim - or inside it.

The sting wears off and the victim starts crawling around again. But it's too late.

When the eggs hatch, the baby wasps eat their host from the inside out.

There are even wasps that lay their eggs inside the larvae of other wasps!

Chapter 5:
Human habitats

Your body is full of horrible habitats too, from the top of your head to the gaps between your toes!

Hairy habitats

Headlice are small for insects. They only grow up to 3 mm long, but they are bigger than most creatures that live on our bodies.

Headlice might make you itch as they slurp blood from your scalp, but they do no real harm.

It's hard to spot headlice, but you might spot their eggs, known as 'nits'.

There are even creatures small enough to hide in your eyelashes! Eight-legged Demodex mites are ten times smaller than headlice, which means they can hide in the tiny holes that eyelashes and eyebrows sprout from.

At night, they wander around your face, creeping back inside the holes to lay eggs.

They are harmless, although some people are **allergic** to their poop.

Demodex mite

Micro-habitats

Your skin is teeming with microbes. Although they are far too small to see, around one million are crammed on to every patch as large as a fingertip!

Your belly button is one of your body's most crowded habitats. Scientists once tested 60 belly buttons and discovered more than 2000 types of microbes living there.

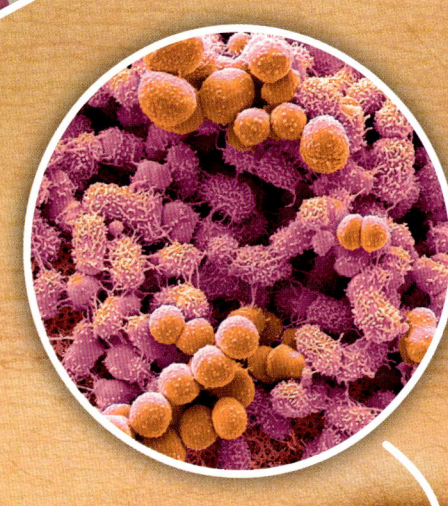

It's a jungle in here!

Just like animals, microbes like places that are warm, wet and full of food. This makes our intestines the perfect habitat! Billions of microbes live in your gut, helping you to digest your food in return for a place to live.

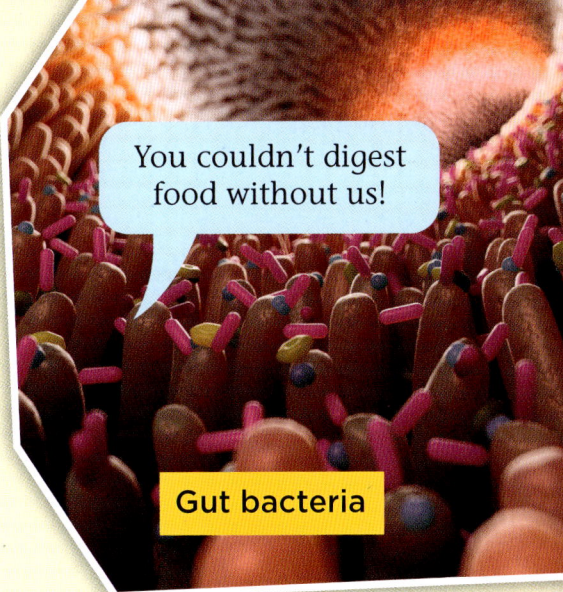

You couldn't digest food without us!

Gut bacteria

Meet the neighbours

- Tiny fungi love to live on warm, sweaty skin, such as the skin between your toes. They digest dead skin, which can cause itching.
- Pinworms live inside millions of people, especially children. They don't cause any harm but may give you an itchy bottom.

Pinworm

Horrible habitats everywhere

Visit any corner of our planet – no matter how horrible – and you'll find living things.

From murky mines to toxic mud, there is no habitat too stinky, too dark, too deep or too deadly to be home to something!

Don Juan Pond

This pond in Antarctica contains the world's saltiest water. Scientists have found evidence that microbes may live in the mud at the bottom.

In the Kidd Creek Mine, Canada, microbes have been found 2.4 kilometres below the surface. They feed on solid rock!

Yum, yum!

If creatures can survive in Earth's most horrible habitats, there might be living things in other parts of our solar system. We already know that water bears and certain microbes can survive in space! Perhaps we will one day find microbes at the bottom of super-salty ponds on Mars.

Glossary

allergic	when your body reacts to a harmless substance as if it is a germ or a poison
average	a typical example of something
blubber	the fat of mammals that live in the sea, such as whales and seals
coral reefs	underwater structures made by tiny living things, called corals, the reef includes all of the other creatures that live there
digest	break food down to use its energy and nutrients
digestive juices	fluids made by a plant or animal to help it digest (break down) food
fungus	a member of a group of living things that absorb food from the surface they grow on, and reproduce by making spores
gills	the organ that allows fish and some amphibians to soak up oxygen from water
immune	when your body can easily fight off a certain germ or poison so it does not make you ill
intestines	part of the body used to digest food
mate	a breeding partner
microbes	tiny living things that can only be seen through a microscope
mucus	a slimy substance made by living things for protection
parasites	living things that live in or on another living thing, taking resources such as food and water, but not giving anything back
predators	animals that hunts and eats other animals

sewage waste, such as human poo and wee, that is carried away from houses and buildings by pipes

spores tiny particles that some living things make and release so they can reproduce; unlike eggs or seeds, a spore can grow into a new living thing without being fertilised

submersibles small underwater boats or crafts, made for exploring rather than travelling or living on

trench a long, narrow and deep 'valley' on the ocean floor

Index

anemones 19
Antarctica 4, 6–7, 36
belly button 34
coral reefs 21
cowpats 14–15
deep-sea vents 4, 11
detritivores 12–13
ecosystems 3
fungus 14–15, 29, 35
Goldilocks planet 4
hat-thrower fungus 14–15
humans 8, 16, 32–33
intestines 28, 35
Kidd Creek Mine 37
Mariana trench 10
microbes 25, 34–35, 36–37

mountain habitats 8–9
mucus 19
nettles 19
parasites 26–27, 30–31
pitcher plants 22–23
predators 17, 20, 22, 23, 26
Sahara desert 5
salty habitats 6, 24–25, 36, 37
sewers 17
solar system 37
spores 14, 29
stings 18–19, 30
teeth cleaning 20–21
toxic habitats 24–25, 36
volcano crater 25

Now answer the questions …

1. Look at the question at the start of page 6. Why might page 5 make you long for an icy drink?

2. Use the chart on page 8 to find out how a human would feel in the habitat of a Himalayan wolf and a large-eared pika (page 9).

3. What do giant isopods (page 10) and sea cucumbers (page 13) have in common?

4. Why does a hat-thrower fungus need to get its spores out of the cowpat it grows on? (page 14)

5. On page 28, why is the word 'caterpillar' inside quotation marks?

6. What might happen to a baby lungworm after it has been launched on to fresh grass? (page 15)

7. Why do you think many creatures steer clear of dead, rotting plants and animals? (page 12)

8. What does the author mean when she says most fish would turn to ice if they swam in the deep oceans around Antarctica? (page 6)

9. What do you think the made-up word 'Bee-licious!' means? Why has the author used this made-up word here? (page 18)

10. What features do all the habitats in this book have in common?

Picnic

Level 2 – Red

Helpful Hints for Reading at Home

The graphemes (written letters) and phonemes (units of sound) used throughout this series are aligned with Letters and Sounds. This offers a consistent approach to learning whether reading at home or in the classroom.

HERE IS A LIST OF PHONEMES FOR THIS PHASE OF LEARNING. AN EXAMPLE OF THE PRONUNCIATION CAN BE FOUND IN BRACKETS.

Phase 2			
s (sat)	a (cat)	t (tap)	p (tap)
i (pin)	n (net)	m (man)	d (dog)
g (go)	o (sock)	c (cat)	k (kin)
ck (sack)	e (elf)	u (up)	r (rabbit)
h (hut)	b (ball)	f (fish)	ff (off)
l (lip)	ll (ball)	ss (hiss)	

Phase 3 Set 6			
j (jam)	v (van)	w (win)	x (mix)

Phase 3 Set 7			
y (yellow)	z (zoo)	zz (buzz)	qu (quick)

HERE ARE SOME WORDS WHICH YOUR CHILD MAY FIND TRICKY.

Phase 2 Tricky Words			
the	to	I	know
go	into		

TOP TIPS FOR HELPING YOUR CHILD TO READ:

• Allow children time to break down unfamiliar words into units of sound and then encourage children to string these sounds together to create the word.

• Encourage your child to point out any focus phonics when they are used.

• Read through the book more than once to grow confidence.

• Ask simple questions about the text to assess understanding.

• Encourage children to use illustrations as prompts.

This book focuses on the phonemes /x/, /y/ and /zz/ and is a red level 2 book band.

Can you say this sound and draw it with your finger?

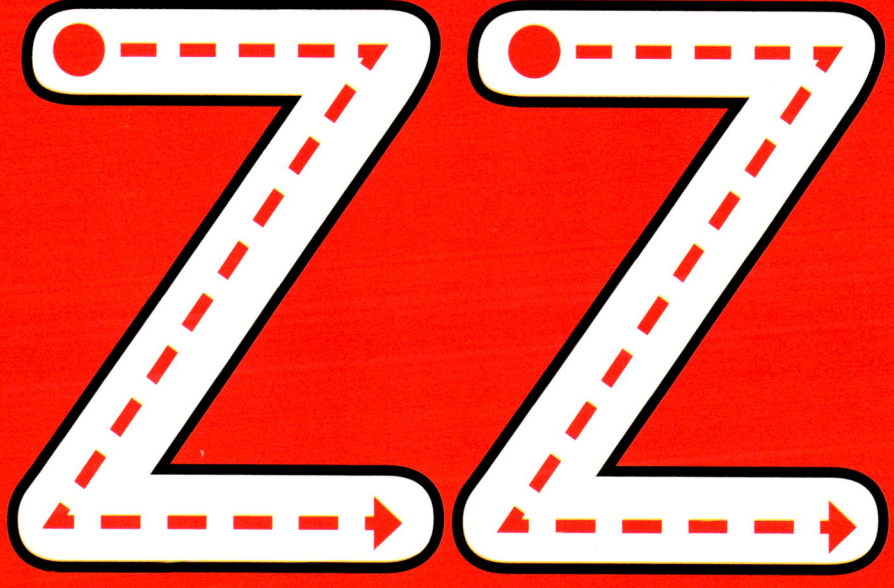

Get the picnic mat. We can sit!

Not yet! It will buzz off.

Get a can of fizz pop.

Get the big fig. Yum!

Get the jam.

Get the bap.

Put the jam in the bap. Yes!

Get the nuts. Yum!

Get the picnic box in, Max!

©This edition published in 2023. First published in 2021.
BookLife Publishing Ltd.
King's Lynn, Norfolk PE30 4LS, UK

ISBN 978-1-83927-896-9

All rights reserved. Printed in China. A catalogue record for this book is available from the British Library.

Picnic
Written by William Anthony
Designed by Amy Li

An Introduction to BookLife Readers...

Our Readers have been specifically created in line with the London Institute of Education's approach to book banding and are phonetically decodable and ordered to support each phase of the Letters and Sounds document.

Each book has been created to provide the best possible reading and learning experience. Our aim is to share our love of books with children, providing both emerging readers and prolific page-turners with beautiful books that are guaranteed to provoke interest and learning, regardless of ability.

BOOK BAND GRADED using the Institute of Education's approach to levelling.

PHONETICALLY DECODABLE supporting each phase of Letters and Sounds.

EXERCISES AND QUESTIONS to offer reinforcement and to ascertain comprehension.

CLEAR DESIGN to inspire and provoke engagement, providing the reader with clear visual representations of each non-fiction topic.

AUTHOR INSIGHT:
WILLIAM ANTHONY

Despite his young age, William Anthony's involvement with children's education is quite extensive. He has written over 60 titles with BookLife Publishing so far, across a wide range of subjects. William graduated from Cardiff University with a 1st Class BA (Hons) in Journalism, Media and Culture, creating an app and a TV series, among other things, during his time there.

William Anthony has also produced work for the Prince's Trust, a charity created by HRH The Prince of Wales, that helps young people with their professional future. He has created animated videos for a children's education company that works closely with the charity.

PHASE 3 /x/ /y/ /zz/

This book focuses on the phonemes /x/, /y/ and /zz/ and is a red level 2 book band.

Image Credits Images are courtesy of Shutterstock.com. With thanks to Getty Images, Thinkstock Photo and iStockphoto. Cover – Nataliia Pyzhova, New Africa, Olga Pink, stockcreations, p4–5 – S_Photo, Littlekidmom, p6–7 – P Maxwell Photography, Spalnic, ElenaYakimov, Gita Kulinitch Studio, p8–9 – Swetlana Wall, PeJo, p10–11 – Creativa Images, BestPhotoStudio.

BookLife Non-Fiction Readers

9781839278938

9781839278921

9781839278945

9781839278952

9781839278976

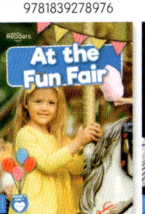
9781839278969

9781839278990

9781839278983

9781839279010

9781839279003

9781839279027

9781839279034

9781839279058

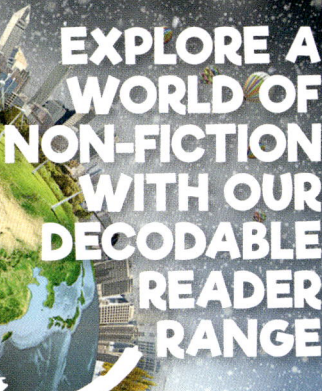
9781839279041

EXPLORE A WORLD OF NON-FICTION WITH OUR DECODABLE READER RANGE

MORE COMING SOON

BookLife PUBLISHING

The BookLife Readers begin with the very basics of **phonetically decodable reading**. Starting with the earliest step of **CVC** words – words comprising a consonant, a vowel and a consonant – and building on this combination slowly, the reader follows a prescribed format taken directly from the recognised **Letters and Sounds** educational document.

By aligning our books with Letters and Sounds, we offer our readers a consistent approach to learning, whether at home or in the classroom. Books levelled as 'a' are an introduction to the band. Readers can advance to 'b' where graphemes are consolidated and further graphemes are introduced. The illustrations guide the reader, helping to deliver reading progression through the scheme in a **colourful** and **exciting** way. As a reader moves through the book band levels, the page numbers, level of repetition and sentence structure complexity all advance at a rate which **encourages development** without halting enjoyment.

To find out more about this exciting new reading scheme, visit **www.booklife.co.uk**

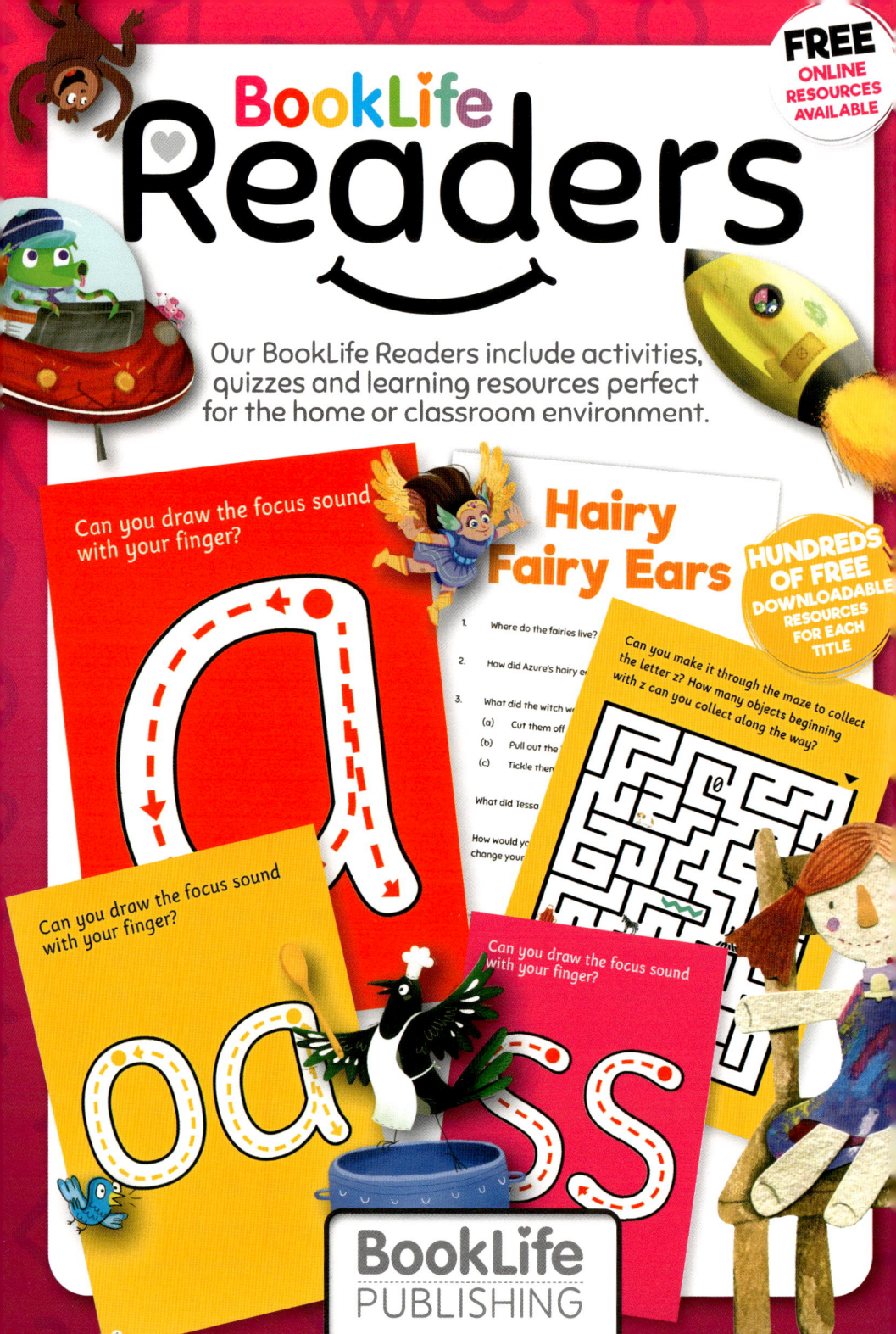